Win Competitions Online:

A Competitors Guide

David Fuentes has been successfully comping for many years, winning heaps of prizes and thousands of pounds worth of free stuff, all from the click of a button. He started out with a dream of winning his way to riches. He is now a force to be reckoned with, winning the cream of the crop must-have gadgets and gizmos whilst getting to experience many money-can't-buy prizes. After years of learning the tricks of the trade, he has now compiled this guide to help those of you who would like to do just that, to follow in his footsteps as it were and pave your own way to untold pleasures. The world is a compers oyster; where will you find your pearl?

Copyright

Win Competitions Online: A Competitors Guide (Second Edition)

Copyright 2015 David Fuentes

All rights reserved. No part of this publication may be reproduced, stored in a retrieval system, or transmitted in any form or by any means, electronic, photocopying, recording or otherwise, without the prior permission in writing of the author, or as expressly permitted by law. The author has used his best endeavours to ensure that any website addresses referred to in this book, or any book in the whole of the Win Competitions Online series are correct and active at the time of publication. However, the author can accept no responsibility for the websites and can make no guarantee that a site will remain live or that the content will remain relevant, decent or safe. For further information please visit www.wincompetitionsonline.com.

Acknowledgements

With Special Thanks To: Nicole Vardon, my editor for all your help and grammar checking. Thomas Phipps for the inspired cover designs. I hope this series of books acts as a good platform for your future career. My parents for their ongoing support; I could not have done it without you. And last but not least; Compers and Promoters who continue to improve and strive in the world of online competitions. Let's hope you all have many more wins to come.

Second Edition Note: Time changes everything. I hope to keep all of my fans, both old and new, abreast of current trends and changes in the world of comping. With this second edition of my first original book I have improved on the overall quality of the content, whilst vastly increasing the quantity of Grade A information crammed into this volume in the series with up to date and current knowledge that I can bring to you all; happy comping.

Congratulations!!

Thank you for purchasing this competitors guide to winning competitions online; you are now one step closer to being a big prize winner. Written in easy to digest segments, I hope to introduce you to your very own Lady Luck and show you that comping can be both an enjoyable and lucrative hobby. This book is your essential guide to take with you on a journey into the world of comping and will be your key to a fortune. It will provide you with vital information for successfully comping, full to the brim with invaluable key tips that will help you avoid some of the pitfalls made by newbie compers. This book will help you get started in comping and will allow you to get to grips with some of the key search and entry methods that are available to you freely across the web whilst saving you time, hassle and a good chunk of your hard earned cash in the process, making those precious pennies stretch even further than you ever dreamed possible. This is your first step; now let's begin your journey...

Contents

- Contents, Terms & Acronyms PP 05-06

- Section 1: Let's Get Started PP 07-18

- Section 2: Tricks Of The Trade PP 19-41

- Section 3: The Buck Stops Here PP 42-46

- Section 4: Social Networking PP 47-58

- Appendix PP 59

- Further Reading PP 60

Terms & Acronyms

Comper: Someone who enters competitions

Promoter: The prize provider

A Gold Mine: A source of multiple wins

SBC: Skill based competition

NPN: No purchase necessary

WEM: Winning email

PN: Prize notification

WC: Winning call

TB: Tie breaker

PD: Prize draw

EF: Entry form

CD: Closing date

Caution: **"Don't quit your day job"** Competitions should only be used as an extra source of holidays, cash prizes and nights out… plus the occasional shopping spree.

Let's Get Started

"What Is Luck?"

Wikipedia defines Luck as "good fortune which occurs beyond ones control, without regard to ones will, intention or desired result". Whether you believe in four leaf clovers or a lucky rabbits foot all of us have experienced the effects of luck in our daily lives; some achieving great fortune, others sheer misfortune. Whether it can be justified or not, the scales of justice will tip one way or another. Life in itself is fraught with superstitions as to why these occurrences come to be; from the Mayans and ritual sacrifices for a good harvest, to modern day Britain's being careful not to step under a ladder to avoid its ill effects. They have always been present and will continue to do so. I myself am a great advocate of the old adage "we make our own luck", and that's where this book comes in…

"Get The Ball Rolling"

The first step is always the hardest. Start your journey off on the right track by adding yourself to a few large and small company email lists. These can be well known magazines that hold regular competitions, for example, Instyle magazine (instyle.co.uk), restaurants and coffee shops like Pizza Express (Pizzaexpress.com) and Costa (Costa.co.uk) or other retail and leisure destinations, for exclusive subscriber only prizes and freebies. There are a whole heap of great prizes on offer; you simply need to know where to look. You can also use Google or other search engines to hunt down your desired prizes using such terms as "Win an iPad", or just ask your friends and fellow compers to find out more about the mysterious world of online comping.

"Your Very Own Lady Luck"

Beat the odds by entering as many competitions as you can; "it is a numbers game", so the more the merrier. An ideal way of doing this is by setting yourself a goal amount of competitions to be done per day, per week, per month... and so on. Use some sort of tally system. What some fellow compers do is they use a handheld clicker; it acts as a tracker of entry amounts whilst also being a rewarding motivational helper, to keep you entering. Do what works best, but remember, you have to be "in it to win it" and perseverance is a key part of what it takes to be a successful comper, that and a good brush with Lady Luck. She can be a harsh mistress at times but if you treat her well she will reward you, sooner rather than later, with heaps of fantastic prizes.

"Cut Out The Spam"

Opt out of all third party emails when entering any prize draw style competitions and especially when it comes to survey sites; believe me, you would not want any of that hassle. You can also set up an extra email account through Google (mail.google.com) and Hotmail (hotmail.com) or whichever takes your fancy, for all your countless hours of comping activity. This will make sure that your standard email address does not get clogged up with unwanted spam. Should it become overrun, despite your best efforts, sign up to Unroll (Unroll.me) to "Clean up your Inbox". This is a great site that has a number of useful features such as putting all your best emails in a daily roll up, bringing all the good stuff together whilst easily allowing you to unsubscribe from those pesky nuisances filling up your inbox, making it easier to find your winning emails (WEM's).

"Flights Not Included"

Always check what you are comping for. Some hotel promoters give you the 7 night stay in the luxury accommodation but do not fork out for the travel, transfers, meals and other amenities. Make sure you have some cash behind you, just in case you are caught short; it's no use being a bit strapped for cash in this situation. Also beware of time shares, there are a lot of cases where people have been suckered into deals that were too good to be true, tempted by their own greed to reap the benefits of a "once in a lifetime" opportunity and pressurised to part with their hard earned money on fool hardy investments. As a final note, make sure you have a valid passport with at least 6 months left on it at all times, this will also come in handy when the time comes.

"Dodgy Dealers"

Anyone with an internet connection can make a website these days. They could be round the corner running the site from a local deli on the other side of the world in a plush office, or even sitting next to you in a coffee shop hacking into your private data via Bluetooth. You must stay safe online by checking some basics like, for example: does the website look genuine and do they respect your privacy by not passing your personal information onto undisclosed third parties? Always trust your gut if you feel suspicious. Your best bet is to go with websites that are either well known brands run by large companies or for competitions that a lot of other people have already entered. For extra help, fellow compers run groups on Facebook and other sites that can help you stay safe in the world of online competitions.

"Multiplicity"

Enter competitions with multiple prizes will drastically improve your chances of winning, especially if there are more prizes to be won than there are people entering (it can happen); a great tactic and well worth trying for a decent prize. These can range from minor items like coffee machines and blenders to the extravagant major prizes of all-inclusive holidays to the Seychelles and fast cars. You could also get your friends and family to enter as well, that way if they win they might take you along for the ride. Some entry apps give you extra entries as well for doing so. This is especially good when say, you are allowed to share the competition with your followers and for each follower who enters through your special coded link you get 1 or more bonus entries. It's worth playing around with to see if you fare better this way; at the end of the day it's your call.

"Correct Is Key"

Always enter your correct details. If you are in any doubt that your information will not be in safe hands or that the competition appears to be suspect in some way, shape or form, then you can either carry out some background checks on the company i.e. through social media groups with other compers, or move onto another competition entirely: better safe than sorry. Also, double check any form fillers that you may be using, an incorrect digit or spelling error could cost you big time. Sometimes the company has to pass your details onto a third party media agency or other supplier contracted to give out the prizes where certain information can be lost in transit due to administrative errors. Contact the promoter if your prize takes longer than 28 days to show up as they might have encountered a few problems along the way; or be trying to pull a fast one.

"The Sky's The Limit"

There are companies and special websites out there that run competitions with no cap on entry numbers or ridiculous allowances for entries per person i.e. you can enter up to 100 times (per phone number). I advise that you do not waste your time with these competitions; the chances of winning the prize would be slim, to say the least. If you would enter the competition a hundred times to increase your overall odds of winning it, then there is nothing to stop someone else from doing the same. Unless it is a life changing "genuine" prize from a respectable source that may be worth a punt, I say leave it be. It pays to be realistic in comping; you will end up wasting less time chasing rainbows and winning more pots of gold instead.

"The Small Print"

As a general rule, you should always check the terms and conditions of any prize draw or skill based competition that you enter; it is certainly best that you know what you are getting into before entering. By checking the small print you can see, for a start, if the competition is still running. It also allows you to double check to see if there is any indication that you will be unwittingly harassed i.e. by an energy company wanting you to switch supplier. Always make sure you are eligible to win the prize (e.g. age and gender restrictions) sometimes you may have to ask the promoter for their terms of entry if they are not present or you could simply ask them to clear up any confusions you may have. Don't be afraid to make an enquiry should it be necessary. Overall only enter if you want the prize that is on offer or know someone who would like it as a gift.

"The Betting Bug"

Entering free online competitions has been likened to other forms of gambling such as slot machines and poker as addictive, it certainly has been for me. Unfortunately as with all addictions they can have some less appealing somewhat negative side effects, like spending all day (and night) comping or getting yourself into a stressful state when the big win just doesn't seem to be coming your way. Make sure you don't fall into the trap of comping for compings sake. Give yourself a timeout now and again, especially when it comes to the Christmas season where comping can go into overdrive due to daily advent calendar style competitions. Keep yourself fit and healthy and stay safe online and offline in your daily lives. Do not take any unnecessary risks i.e. to get that perfect photo shot for a skill based entry and above all enjoy the ride.

Tricks Of The Trade

"Be Resourceful"

Every trade has its tricks and it is my job to show you those of a comper. First off you should always make use of competition directories such as The Prize Finder (Theprizefinder.com) or as a nice alternative UK Wins (Ukwins.co.uk) for quick to find competitions. There are a variety of others but in general you will be finding the same competitions and may well disqualify yourself by entering the competition more than is allowed by the promoter. It is best to keep to your favourite directories where you can track your entries more proficiently. This will reduce your overall time spent looking for competitions and can be a god send for all your comping activity. Features range from split listings showing you the prizes you want to win to types of competition i.e. standard prize draw or creative entry. The world is a compers oyster.

"Comping On The Go"

Keep up with your daily fill of competition entries when you are out on the go, even whilst on holiday, if you fancy it. With unlimited mobile internet connections, free WIFI in cafes; libraries, fast food restaurants and pubs, you can now enter online (and offline) competitions wherever and whenever the comping bug strikes (well, maybe not in a tunnel)... This time can be used for filling out some postal entries. Before making a move, check that you are not missing out on some possible photo opportunities to grab some low entry prizes. Take a quick search on skill based entries i.e "photo" and "video" on the directories or you could ask your comping friends through social media sites and other chat groups.

"Fill Up On AutoFill"

This will be your essential piece of comping equipment, the ratchet in your comping tool belt. AutoFill is available on the Google Chrome web browser; check out other browsers for alternatives. Just add this helpful piece of kit to your toolbar and you will notice a great improvement in your online comping activity. This add-on saves your data for online entry forms so that you don't have to waste time needlessly entering your details over and over again, which can get quite tiring and somewhat de-motivating in the long run. AutoFill can also be used for multiple personal profiles; you can store your partner or child's details if need be. Credit card information can also be stored for creative and other non-comping purchases, for example a massive inflatable palm tree and a few other inflatable goodies for the creation of a Caribbean style setting.

"Cut Out The Leg Work"

If Google AutoFill just doesn't cut the mustard and you are left wanting something a little bit meatier, then embrace the power of RoboForm (Roboform.com). This is an advanced piece of comping artillery that works in a very similar way to AutoFill by safely storing your address and other personal data but with a click of a button, fills out any forms you need filling, with customizable data tabs to boot. "RoboForm Data is secured with military-grade AES 256 encryption", so you can rest easy knowing that your data is safe and secure, not only that but it's free to use and can be utilized across many different platforms should you need to. There's also a password generator that lets you customize you own secure passwords to use across the web.

"Pick 'A' Mix"

With thousands of competitions available through the internet, in magazines, newspapers and beyond, you may be left a little overwhelmed by it all. Make sure you tick that dream prize off your bucket list by entering a mix of competitions that are closing soon, ending in the near future and finishing in a few months or so. That way if you are too busy to enter any competitions for a while or the internet's down on your break to Monaco, you will still have a chance of winning a great prize every day. Keep in mind that some prizes are time and/or location specific, some even require you to confirm attendance within a short period after being notified, usually about a week or so but sometimes within an hour. If you are not available and can't make use of the prize, let some other compers know about it instead; spread the comping love.

"X Marks The Spot"

There's no point in rushing a multiple choice question only to end up entering the wrong answer, ticking the wrong box, or mucking it all up with an error in your contact details: "if in doubt, work it out". The best route for this is via a quick Google search. The forums come in handy as well, i.e. you can put the question / the whole prize description into a search engine then "+ money saving expert" or "+ hot uk deals", click a suitable link and hey presto, your answer is revealed. Most directories cover the answers to a lot of competitions out there so it's always worth a go if you are struggling to figure it out. Some competitions have no one right answer; they are open to interpretation, say through a creative picture entry, your best bet with these types of competitions is to make sure you follow the terms and conditions and don't run the risk of being disqualified.

"Season's Greetings"

Christmas, Easter and even Thanksgiving! Special themed promotions come about in abundance around the holiday season, in order to attract new and old customers to the company websites and social media pages. Advent calendars with daily prize draws around Christmas are the norm, so keep a look out on the directories, mark down the sites that are participating and enter away. You can also bookmark select websites in your browser to help you keep track of the best daily competitions, saving you your time and sanity, without having to trawl through the less appealing low value prizes. Unusual events such as Movember and National Chip Week also have great competitions as well, with prizes being given out in conjunction with the ongoing theme.

"The Creative Comper"

Bring out your creative side with the likes of slogans, recipes and other skill based competitions; simple, fun and worth every penny. These types of competitions are harder to enter than the standard quiz style/ multiple choice competitions and so receive fewer entries, therefore increasing your odds of winning. The more creative you are the better, but beware: in order to win at these types of competitions you are really going to have to push the boat out. A fellow comper won a trip to New York by dressing up as the statue of liberty, using cardboard cut outs and what looked like a nice pair of curtains, backdrop of the American flag included. It was judged the best by the promoter and off she went, jetting off on an all expenses paid trip of a lifetime.

"Validate Your Entry"

Some promoters require you to reply to an email validation code/link after you have entered their competition; this helps the promoter to cut down on emails from spammers and combat robotic entries. Make sure you reply via the link or you will not be entered. An example of this is the gadget website T3.com, which requires you to reply via a validation link that they send to you after entering each competition. Beware of clicking links claiming to be prizes from unknown sources; this could lead to computer viruses or other malicious effects. Another point to bear in mind, is not to disqualify yourself, say by entering from multiple accounts from the same I.P address or by doing something else that may negatively affect your chances of winning.

"The Never Ending Competition"

In general you should stay away from competitions that run endlessly / more than a few months. There is very little chance of yourself being the lucky winner due to the sheer numbers of entrants and resulting entries, the best competitions are those that last say 1-2 weeks, or if you are "lucky", a day or so, of course searching tactics for low entry competitions come into play here. Some sites such as ThePrizeFinder.com tell you when the competition ends whilst also informing you of when it has been posted, at least on their own site. Unfortunately some promoters do not list the closing date for their competition, some scammers may well miss that one out as well, and in this case I would advise asking them if you are in doubt that your entry would still be valid.

"Slogan Showdown"

Get those creative juices flowing with the aid of File Hippo (Filehippo.com). This will help you compose your very own slogans for caption competitions. Simply type in a word into their "words that rhyme with" section and it will soon come up with some great ideas. Compers News (Compersnews.com) also has a database of winning "Chestnut" slogans that can be applied to any creative competitions that you may come across. Chestnut slogans are those that have been used by fellow compers to consistently win prizes with varying levels of success due to their witty and on the ball summations. Of course creative comping is about coming up with your own "Stevie" wonders, but should you need a quick fix or some creative inspiration, these will surely come in handy.

"When Lightning Strikes"

I have personally won a small fortunes worth of prizes from radio and newspaper sites, and most recently from social media pages, where the competitions are poorly advertised by the promoter, ipso facto there are less people entering and so there is a greater chance of winning them; after all, prize draws can be a numbers game. Find your "gold mine" by searching high and low across directories and niche company websites, chart your success and keep track of where your prizes are coming from for correlations between the areas you are focused on, the amount of effort you are putting in and the end results of some fantastic prizes for yourself and the rest of your family, who will appreciate all the lovely treats you will end up giving them.

"Dear Diary"

Keep track of those important dates; make sure you know when the event is scheduled, or when the competition is closing, if you really want to win the prize but say you haven't purchased the product to be eligible to enter and win. I have missed out on a number of prizes because of mixed up dates, or simply because I couldn't attend them all, which have included tickets to gigs, film premieres and other events. The thing is once you get to my level of comping, it does not really matter to you as much about the odd festivals and other bits and pieces that you have missed out on, there will always be more wins, and on a daily basis. But still, in the early days you will want to win and go to as much as you can to fuel your comping bugs appetite, a thirst for comping glory. Just don't go too mad on the open bars, been there, done that, won the t-shirt.

"We Have A Winner"

One thing you should always do on a daily basis, if you can, is to check your emails for prizes: some competitions must be replied to by the end of the day or sooner in order to receive your prize. I had to reply to the Guardian newspaper by 5pm that same day of receiving the email notification so I could be booked onto a bee-keeping masterclass, me and my partner were glad I did. Also do not forget to check your social media pages should you receive a winning notification from them, adjust your profiles settings for help. Remember, some competition sites such as winsomething.co.uk only send you a single email notification and should you not reply within the allocated time frame (usually a week or so) you will end up forfeiting your prize of a lifetime.

"Log Your Progress"

Some of the best compers in the game keep an active and up to date competition log to make sure they do not enter the same competition more than once unless they are allowed too or feel they can get away with it. Some people also log their wins, especially when it comes to organizing which promoters they may need to chase up for some of their prizes. Unfortunately with some promoters, if you do not push them for an answer, your prize will get lost in administration. Some of my own prizes have taken many months of pestering and perseverance to finally arrive but a few were just a lost cause. Of course you can take it further by getting in contact with the advertising standards agency (ASA) for help, but some prizes such as say a t-shirt or mug are simply not worth the effort.

"Trackers & Cookies"

Some competition directories such as ThePrizeFinder.com and many others like UkCompetitions.com use cookies (not the dunking kind) and other pieces of software to show you which competitions you have entered through them and which ones are still left to enter before the closing date. To make use of this competition tracking and logging feature; you simply have to sign up as a free member. This helps you keep track of your entries and allows you to keep within the rules of the competition; just make sure you are not entering the same competitions through different competition directories. Certain competitions are repeated across the board, especially the really juicy ones that you just can't wait to sink your teeth into.

"Survey Sites"

In recent times, newspapers, radio sites, lads magazines and other promoters have begun to outsource to other specialized companies for their promotional giveaway needs. They have given permission to sites such as My Offers (Myoffers.co.uk) and a plethora of other survey sites to pick up the slack. These sites literally receive millions of entries and so the odds of winning are extremely low, pretty much like the national lottery and premium bonds. That is not to say someone does not win them, but I would prefer better odds. You also run the risk of receiving premium cost text messages should you mistakenly sign up to the service through a check box on a competition entry, not to mention the extra mountains of spam that will soon be flooding your inbox. By all means check the sites out; after all you never know until you give them a go.

"Alternative Routes"

I find that internet comping works best for me: it is quick, easy and, if you have a good electricity / broadband provider (that doesn't cut out on you too frequently), the cheapest way to successfully enter your daily competitions. Text and phone entries on daytime television shows are one of the many other routes available to the newbie comper; you could also do postal entries although these can consume more of your time they are certainly at least half the cost of a text/phone entry and second class stamps are great if the competition does not end for a few weeks. You could also enter a few competitions at one of the many expos and conventions that are out there; do what works best for you. Don't forget, there are new apps and sites springing up all the time.

"Game Shows"

Another route you may wish to go down, especially if you are up for a fun and entertaining experience is that of the game/quiz show contestant. There is a whole host of sites online devoted to finding the next lucky big time winner, give Beonscreen.com and Ukgameshows.com a try, but also keep listening out to your favorite shows for application details; you could be their next big winner. You can also be in the audience of some of your favorite shows, which are not limited to just these varieties. Check out Applausestore.com or Lostintv.com, which can also be used for applying to shows for a whole range of great nights out, giving you a firsthand experience of how they are shot and played out: this will give you a tactical advantage when it comes to facing the cameras once the call comes in to make your dreams a reality.

"Speed Up Your CPU"

If you are sick of your computers slow performance and want to speed up your CPU (central processing unit), then make use of Ccleaner from Filehippo.com to rid yourself of any unnecessary (cache) baggage. It may also be worth investing in a larger ram, deleting unnecessary user accounts and freeing up your hard drive of any old programs and documents, you could just buy a brand spanking new model or start entering more computer competitions and if you are at work best make friends with the I.T crowd. Also, keep your internet security up to date; any bugs you may pick up on your journey through the web will slow down your computers abilities, plus as time goes on larger files can really put a drain on its processing power.

"Picture Perfect"

Some competitions require more cunning than others; make way for the powerhouse that is Tineye (Tineye.com). This site works by finding the source of images for "where is this" picture competitions, those that require you to enter the location of the image as the answer. Working best on landscapes it searches the images Uniform Resource Locator (URL) for related links and information. The basics for use are: right click any image on the web, "copy the Images URL" and submit to Tineye. You can also upload an image direct from your hard drive, you will be given a series of websites that are linked to the image of which should contain the answer. If you are still stuck, Google the landmarks in the picture for example a local church or railway signage for more help. Keep at it; the harder and more challenging ones receive far fewer entries.

"Chestnut Slogans"

Tie-breaker style competitions are all the rage with promoters cashing in on the craze, whether via a caption competition that requires you to come up with a witty pun for a photo, or a one sentence reason why you should go on an all-inclusive holiday to Jamaica. A rule of thumb would be to mention the promoter, the prize and make it rhyme. Although some promoters can get sick of this, having every entrant under the sun come up with the same old corny answer, if you can think of something that is unique to you or that stands out in a positive way, you will stand a better chance of winning. After all, it is not all about numbers, especially when it comes to skill based competitions with a judge looking for the best match to their own criteria. Follow these steps and you are well on your way to winning some fantastic life changing prizes.

The Buck Stops Here

"No Purchase Necessary"

Raid your local supermarket shelves for competitions in newspapers, on soup cartons, health magazines, you name it, take note of the websites on your phone and enter away. If the competition requires a purchase be sure to keep your receipt as proof, in case you win. When the promoter rings make sure you know where you put it. A filing system would certainly come in handy; it beats a last minute rummage through your purse for a winning ticket. Some creative competitions also require you to purchase the promoters product in order to enter say, by including it in a Hawaiian scene you set up at home. This has worked well for me in the past. Always take a few extra shots without the product for greater re-use value in other competitions.

"No Time To Spare"

The Prize Centre (no longer active) and other "automated entry services" such as We Win 4 U (wewin4u.co.uk) can enter you into 250+ competitions a month with charges from only £1.95 a week, but the big question is: are they worth the investment? With a few quick calculations, it would work out as £101.40 to enter around 3000 competitions that year, depending on the prizes, overall odds and if they are not telling porkies, it may be worth a punt. Your best bet is to do a little research on the prize forums and blogs and see what others have to say about them. I personally do not use these sites, plus they do not enter you into creative style and photo competitions which can be a lot more fun to enter than standard prize draws. They do have a lot of "genuine" prize winner stories on their site, but tread with caution and look for unbiased sources elsewhere.

"Prizes For Sale"

Once you start raking in the prizes, you will soon have so many of them that your house will be full to the brim. So instead of renting out a storage unit why not sell your unwanted wins? You can sell tickets through Viagogo (Viagogo.co.uk), household goods on Ebay (Ebay.co.uk) and all others under the sun on Gumtree (Gumtree.com). You can also use social media groups i.e. London selling groups on Facebook. If the giver in you beckons you can give them away to others as birthday or wedding presents, depending on the value, or wait for a sunny day and pop out for a car boot sale. Free Cycle (Freecycle.org) may also be of use, keeping your unwanted items out of landfills and there are always charity shops. If your products are not selling well, try linking your advert to the promoters social media pages or related videos on Youtube (Youtube.com).

"Problem Promoters"

It is unfortunate and extremely frustrating to be the winner of a fabulous competition, anxiously waiting for a whole month (28 days), probably bragging to a few friends, only to not receive the prize, which can be extremely disheartening. Although rare if you have any problems firstly you should email the promoter, to see if they have received your details. Sometimes a little nudge gets results but it's not worth losing your rag over. Try contacting the companies' complaints department to see if that has any effect on the situation. If you are still not getting anywhere with that get onto the Advertising Standards Agency (Asa.org.uk) or the Institute of Promotional Marketing (Theipm.org.uk) for help and advice regarding unfair promotions and advertising.

Social Networking

"I Heard It On The Grapevine"

If you feel you are 'up the creek without a paddle', then it is high time to engage others who may well be able to help you with your problems through online forums and compers communities. There are a lot of great sources to look out for. You could try HotUKDeals (hotukdeals.com), as a logged in member or even as a guest; you can chat under the posts in question and ask any questions you may have. You could also try Money Saving Experts online prize forums (forums.moneysavingexpert.com); great for both on and off topic discussion. You may well find out about competitions that are easy to win or have very few entries. A lot of these sites also double up as competition directories and freebie nirvanas, worth a good rummage when you have the time.

"The Socialite"

Social media sites such as Facebook, Twitter and Instagram are the way forward in comping and the future of online competitions. Long gone are the days of mass postal entries; the future will be a lot more socially focused. Companies are already turning to such specialised competition only sites such as Competwition (Competwition.com); great for hosting a lot of great twitter giveaways and Ninjawin (Ninjawin.com) which can also be utilised for Facebook competitions as well: all for free. Maybe instagram and other types in the future will have their own versions; just keep listening to that competition grapevine. Pay with a Tweet, Facebook sweepstakes and vote-for-me style competitions are also used to increase promoters' sales and brand awareness and it is set to grow so get on the band wagon before it is too late.

"Welcome To The Family"

Not exactly the Mafia, and far less risky, you too can be part of "The Family". The first step to joining a comping community is to hit up the forums and comping blogs which are a brilliant source of knowledge and inspiration. Some of the best are Money Saving Expert (Moneysavingexpert.com): look under the bargains, shopping and freebies section, and as mentioned earlier Hot UK Deals (Hotukdeals.com) with great advice given throughout the site. They are great for giving you the answers to some tricky competition questions; they really do put the effort in. Always remember to post any competitions you find from other sites that may not be covered, contributions are always welcome and no one wants to be a leech; you give a little and get a lot back.

"Share Your Story"

The Prize Finder (Theprizefinder.com) hosts a monthly prize draw for the best and most creative winning stories from within the comping community. These true stories act as an inspiration to fellow compers. You too can help others win their dreams by setting up your own competition blog, or by bragging down the local with a few pints and some great friends. You should always aim to inspire others with your stories not to make them jealous: I would advise spending more time comping, less time gloating. In recent times some compers have been in the media in magazines and newspapers, even on the radio under false, envious headlines that give compers a bad name. Just remember, you will not be able to retire on your daily comping activities but you will improve your life and the lives of those nearest and dearest to you; a great result.

"Courtesy Counts"

Always be kind and courteous when winning any prizes whether large or small, it does not help to come across as unappreciative. Remember to thank the promoter for hosting the competition and for picking you as the lucky winner; who knows, this might carry favour for the next "random" draw or they could upgrade your prize for being so nice. This has happened to me before, enjoying the VIP treatment with free drinks as opposed to standard tickets. This will also give the promoter a good view of the comping community. Some competition promoters actively discourage compers and state that they will not pick a "professional comper" / "serial retweeter" so be aware of this. Lastly, make sure they have received your details; I had to send an email out a few times to get a luxury hamper full of goodies which was a great gift for the partner.

"Two Heads Are Better Than One"

Encourage your friends to join you in the world of comping; having more entries in your favor is a clear winner. Competitions to keep in mind for this are joint holidays and other getaways; some promoters also make this a requirement i.e. bring 3 extra friends with you on a trip to America, this may require them to also sign up to the promoters page for your entry to be eligible. Some sharing competitions, for example ones run on Woobox (Woobox.com) that are greatly used through Facebook or Gleam (Gleam.io) giveaways give you extra entries for each friend that signs up through your unique referral link; some compers share theirs through different groups and forums, you can also share on your own Facebook and Twitter pages, a very social way to win.

"Do It Yourself"

If you are running a company yourself and want to increase your brand awareness and business sales, you can go about hosting your own competition. For those of you who are running a blog, you can create your own giveaway through the quick and easy use of Rafflecopter (Rafflecopter.com) and Random (Random.org) which has a true random number generator to set up a competition and pick a winner. You could also run apps or like and share competitions on Facebook, like and re-tweet to enter competitions on twitter or repost-and-tag-us competitions on instagram. This is great for promoting your business and gaining a few new friends along the way. Some things to look out for are multiple fake accounts used to enter using fake details. If you suspect there has been fowl play it is entirely at your own discretion whether to award to prize to that entrant.

"Tweet, Twitter, Tweeter"

Twitter is one of the fastest growing social networks in the age of social media and promoters have been quick to jump on the band wagon to help promote their latest gadgets and gizmos. They have been able to host competitions that require you to follow them and retweet the relevant competition tweets to enter for prizes, where all you have to do is click the symbols below the retweet and win messages and you are quickly entered to win some great prizes. Compers and promoters can also try out Tweet Deck (Tweetdeck.com) or Hootsuite (Hootsuite.com) which are great for power tweeters, those who cannot get enough of it. For compers who love a little flutter, Competwition (Competwition.com) works great for stand-alone prize draws.

"You've Just Been Facebooked"

Facebook has now opened up to the comping community. Firstly there are like-and-share competitions; these require you to like the promoters page, click 'like' on the relevant prize photo and share the photo with your friends. Make sure your privacy settings are on public for your posts, and remember to comment below the post on their page to let them know you have entered; they may also reply on the comment to let you know you have won. There are also competition apps; just follow the instructions given on the app. Some of the promoters have had problems with people stealing prizes when they ask on their walls for delivery details, so when notified make sure they get your correct information promptly before the prize gets snapped up.

"The 'Vote' Exchange"

For Facebook or other "vote for me" competitions there are a number of websites that allow you to increase your vote amounts, therefore greatly improving your chances of winning. There is a community for exchanging vote. Now, I do not advocate the use of these sites but would like to inform you of what is out there of which include Unlimited-Vote-Exchange on Facebook and the useful Vote Exchange onlineforum (VoteExchange.Niceboard.com). You even have some people who use cheat engines to slow down games in order to get the fastest time on leader boards to win the top prize; check out the Wiki page on Cheat Engines (wiki.cheatengine.org) for more information on that, but tread carefully with it and be warned "cheaters never prosper".

"Reflection"

Why do you enter competitions? Are you enjoying your comping? Have you had some nice surprises or huge life changing wins? It can help you boost your positivity and outlook on comping when you spend some time on positive reflection. It is great during a "dry spell" where you are not winning a lot, rest assured these spells will end quicker if you put more time and effort into your comping. It is great to go over some of the prizes you have won, especially those that wouldn't have been possible had it not been for comping, whether it be film premieres, special events, or holidays you simply could not afford. Sum up your success and see where you would like to take it next, you may wish to get more creative and do more video entries or leave it as a pleasurable time filler on your days off. Happy Comping, and the best of luck to you all.

Useful Links

Ukwins.co.uk	Moneysavingexpert.com
Ukcompetitions.com	Hotukdeals.com
Loquax.co.uk	Theprizefinder.com
Myoffers.co.uk	Getmeaticket.co.uk
Win24.co.uk	Wewin4u.co.uk
Prizewise.co.uk	Competitionhunter.com
Crazycompers.co.uk	Prizebug.co.uk
Facebook.com	Twitter.com
Competwition.com	Theipm.org.uk
Tweetdeck.com	Winspiration.co.uk
Beonscreen.com	Itv.com/beontv
BBC.co.uk/beonashow	Tineye.com
Wordhippo.com	Filehippo.com
Freecycle.org	Asa.org.uk

Further Reading

Blog.loquax.co.uk

Theprizefinder.com/blog

Compersnews.com

Simplyprizes.magazine.co.uk

The Luck Factor

Did You Spot The Gorilla

Available & Upcoming Editions:

Win Competitions Online: The Sky's The Limit

Win Competitions Online: A Promoters Guide

Win Competitions Online: Scam Watch

Win Competitions Online: The Compendium

Win Competitions Online: Deals & Freebies

Printed in Great Britain
by Amazon